☆ American Girl®

Baking

Photography **Nicole Hill Gerulat**

weldon**owen**

Contents

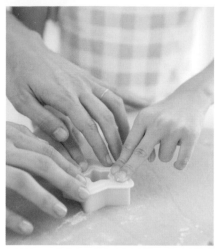

Bake Like You Mean It!

It's easy to understand why baking is so much fun. There's nothing quite as satisfying as measuring and mixing ingredients, putting dough or batter into a hot oven, watching—and smelling!—the transformation during baking, and finally removing delicious sweets from the oven. But the best part is sharing the treats you made with your friends and family.

Whether you follow a recipe step-by-step or add your own unique pizzazz, when you bake with happiness, the results will always be terrific. Perhaps you're the type of baker who sneaks a secret ingredient into the batter, like an extra dash of vanilla extract or a swirl of peanut butter. Or maybe you try to follow a recipe exactly as it is written, so the results are always familiar and yummy. Or do you add your personal touch with bright purple frosting and a scattering of rainbow sprinkles? Whatever your style—whether you're daring, playful, colorful, or classic—baking is a great opportunity to let your personality shine and to create mouthwatering goodies with your own special flair.

Yummy recipes ahead!

In these pages, you'll learn the yummiest baking recipes, from cupcakes to madeleines (little shell-shaped French cakes), cookies to brownies, and a whole lot more. Try Strawberry Cheesecake Cupcakes (page 74) for your next birthday party. Chocolate Madeleines (page 58) are perfect for a tea party, and will impress all of your friends—plus they are super easy to make! Pack a slice or two of Banana–Chocolate Chip Bread (page 96) for your next outdoor adventure, or bake a Golden Layer Cake with Chocolate Frosting (page 116) for your friends or family, just because. Turn the pages to discover the most scrumptious recipes, for any occasion, that will delight any sweet tooth.

Baking with care

Baking is the perfect activity to do with friends and family. Since there are a lot of hot surfaces and sharp objects in the kitchen, always have an adult assist you while baking.

When you see this symbol in the book, it means that you need an adult to help you with all or part of the recipe. Ask for help before continuing.

Tip top baking tips

BE OVEN SMART

Be extra careful when working around a hot oven and hot baking dishes. Always use oven mitts and have an adult help you with taking pans in and out of the oven.

GET HELP WITH APPLIANCES

Electric mixers make mixing batters quick and easy. Always have an adult assist you when using appliances.

STAY ORGANIZED

Staying organized and paying attention are important baking skills. Before you preheat the oven, it's important to read the full recipe and ingredient list. Then it's time to clear a clean surface and lay out all your baking tools and ingredients. Once the food is in the oven, don't forget to set a timer!

The tools you'll need

The recipes in this book use a few basic baking tools. There's no need to go out and buy everything all at once—you can collect tools slowly over time, as you try more and more baking recipes.

★ **Aprons** are handy to help keep your clothes tidy when you are baking.

★ **Cookie cutters** come in all shapes. All-time favorites are butterflies, stars, flowers, and hearts, but use any shape you like.

★ **Cookie sheets**, especially thick, heavy ones, help cookies bake evenly and won't warp in the oven.

★ **Small metal icing spatulas** are good for spreading frosting on cupcakes and cakes. A piping bag fitted with a pastry tip is another way to add frosting or to write fun messages on top of cookies, cakes, and cupcakes.

★ **An electric mixer** makes quick work of batters and frostings, beating egg whites and cream, and more. Always ask an adult for help when using appliances. Use a mixing bowl and wooden spoon or whisk in a pinch.

★ **Madeleine pans** are charming French molds used to create dainty, shell-shaped cakes in a variety of flavors.

★ **Measuring cups and spoons** help you measure your ingredients accurately and easily. Choose graduated sets for dry ingredients and a liquid pitcher for wet ingredients.

★ **Oven mitts or pads** protect your hands from hot pans, oven racks, cookie sheets, and baking dishes. Always ask an adult to help when working near a hot oven or stove.

★ **Parchment paper** is paper that's been treated to give it a nonstick surface. It's used to line cookie sheets and baking pans so that baked goods won't stick. If you don't have parchment paper, you can butter the pans and dust them with flour.

★ **A rubber spatula** is helpful for mixing batters and scraping them into pans, like when you transfer the last bits of batter from a bowl to a muffin pan.

★ **Standard muffin pans,** with 12 cups, are used for the cupcake recipes in this book; for some recipes, you'll need two muffin pans.

Imagination and a good dose of creativity are the two most important baker's tools of all. Have fun!

Cookies

Kissed by chocolate
Instead of using jam, place a chocolate tear-shaped drop into each cookie indent before baking.

Thumbprint Cookies

Use your thumb to create a small indent in the center of these buttery, almond-scented cookies before baking, and fill each one with your favorite fruity, jewel-toned jams, like raspberry, blackberry, or apricot.

2 cups all-purpose flour

½ teaspoon baking powder

¼ teaspoon salt

1 cup (2 sticks) unsalted butter, at room temperature

½ cup sugar

1 teaspoon finely grated orange zest

¾ teaspoon vanilla extract

¼ teaspoon almond extract

½ cup raspberry, apricot, or blackberry jam

 Position 2 racks in the oven so that they are evenly spaced and preheat the oven to 350°F. Line 2 cookie sheets with parchment paper.

In a medium bowl, whisk together the flour, baking powder, and salt. In a large bowl, using an electric mixer, beat the butter and sugar on medium speed until fluffy and pale, about 3 minutes. Add the orange zest, vanilla, and almond extract and beat on medium speed until combined. Turn off the mixer and scrape down the bowl with a rubber spatula. Add half of the flour mixture and mix on low speed just until blended. Add the rest of the flour mixture and mix just until blended. Scrape down the bowl.

Scoop up a rounded tablespoonful of dough, then use your finger to push the dough onto 1 of the prepared cookie sheets. Fill both cookie sheets with dough, spacing the mounds 2 inches apart. You should be able to fit 12 cookies on each cookie sheet.

Dip your thumb in a little flour and use it to make a dent in each ball of dough. Spoon a small amount of jam into each dent. You can vary the types of jam you use to make different flavors of cookies.

Bake the cookies until lightly browned, about 18 minutes. Ask an adult to help you remove the cookie sheets from the oven and set them on wire racks. Let cool for 10 minutes, then use a metal spatula to move the cookies directly to the racks. Let the cookies cool completely and serve.

Chocolate Whoopie Pies

Is it a pie? Is it a cookie? Is it a cake? You won't even care once you take a bite of these awesome choco-licious treats! And who can resist a sweet, gooey marshmallow filling?

COOKIES

6 tablespoons (¾ stick) unsalted butter, at room temperature

½ cup firmly packed light brown sugar

1 large egg

1 teaspoon vanilla extract

¾ cup all-purpose flour

½ cup unsweetened cocoa powder, sifted

½ teaspoon baking soda

⅛ teaspoon salt

FILLING

1 cup marshmallow creme

½ cup powdered sugar, sifted

4 tablespoons (½ stick) unsalted butter, at room temperature

½ teaspoon vanilla extract

 To make the cookies, in a bowl, using an electric mixer, beat the butter and sugar on medium speed until blended, about 1 minute. Add the egg and vanilla and beat until combined. Turn off the mixer and scrape down the bowl with a rubber spatula. Sift the flour, cocoa, baking soda, and salt into a separate bowl, then add to the butter mixture. Mix on low speed just until blended. Cover the bowl with plastic wrap and refrigerate until the dough is firm, about 2 hours.

Position 2 racks in the oven so that they are evenly spaced and preheat the oven to 350°F. Line 2 cookie sheets with parchment paper.

Moisten your hands with water, scoop up a tablespoonful of the dough, and roll the dough between your palms into a ball. Place the ball on a prepared cookie sheet. Repeat with the rest of the dough, evenly spacing the balls on the cookie sheets and flattening them a little. You should have 20 balls.

Bake the cookies until puffed and slightly firm, 8 to 10 minutes, rotating the pans halfway through (ask an adult for help!). Let the cookies cool for 5 minutes, then use a metal spatula to move them directly to wire racks. Let cool.

To make the filling, in a bowl, using an electric mixer, beat the marshmallow creme, powdered sugar, butter, and vanilla on medium speed until smooth.

Turn half of the cookies bottom side up. Use an icing spatula to spread a dollop of the filling on the surface of each upside-down cookie. Top each with a second cookie, placing the flat side onto the filling. Serve right away.

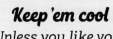

Keep 'em cool
Unless you like your whoopie pies super gooey, you might want to store them in the fridge.

Pinwheel Icebox Cookies

These whimsical cookies are chilled in the refrigerator to help them set into perfect colorful pinwheels. You can make them into cookie pops by inserting ice-pop sticks before baking (follow the directions on page 29).

2 cups all-purpose flour

1 teaspoon baking powder

¼ teaspoon salt

12 tablespoons (1½ sticks) unsalted butter, at room temperature

¾ cup granulated sugar

1 large egg yolk

1½ teaspoons vanilla extract

½ teaspoon red, blue, or green food coloring, plus more as needed

½ teaspoon peppermint extract (optional)

About ½ cup coarse decorating sugar, for rolling (optional)

In a medium bowl, whisk together the flour, baking powder, and salt. In a large bowl, using an electric mixer, beat the butter and granulated sugar on medium speed until fluffy and pale, about 5 minutes. Turn off the mixer and scrape down the bowl with a rubber spatula. Add the egg yolk and vanilla and beat until combined. Add half of the flour mixture and mix on low speed just until blended. Add the rest of the flour mixture and mix just until blended. Scrape down the bowl.

Dump the dough onto a clean work surface and divide it in half. Add one half back to the bowl and sprinkle the food coloring and peppermint extract, if using, over the dough in the bowl, then gently knead until well combined and evenly colored. If the color is not as dark as you'd like, add more food coloring and gently knead it in.

Cut 4 sheets of wax paper, each one about 18 inches long. Set each dough half on the center of a wax paper sheet and use your hands to shape the dough into a rectangle. Cover each piece of dough with a second wax paper sheet and, one at a time, using a rolling pin, roll out the dough halves into 16-by-10-inch rectangles. Remove the wax paper from one side of each dough rectangle and place the colored rectangle over the plain one. Starting from a long side and using the wax paper on the bottom piece of the dough to help, tightly roll the dough into a log. If you like, scatter the coarse sugar on

~ Continued on page 24 ~

Colorful swirls
Make these cookies even more swirl-erific by coloring both halves of the dough with your favorite colors.

~ **Continued from page 23** ~

a rimmed cookie sheet and roll the log in the sugar to coat the outside. Wrap the log tightly in plastic wrap and refrigerate until firm, at least 1 hour or up to overnight.

Preheat the oven to 350°F. Line 2 cookie sheets with parchment paper. Unwrap the dough log and set it on a cutting board. Ask an adult to help you use a knife to trim off the ends, then cut the log crosswise into ¼-inch-thick slices. Place the slices on the prepared cookie sheets, spacing them about 2 inches apart.

When both cookie sheets are full, bake only 1 cookie sheet at a time until the cookies are firm to the touch (ask an adult for help!), about 12 minutes. Ask an adult to help you remove the cookie sheet from the oven and set it on a wire rack. Let cool for 5 minutes, then use a metal spatula to move the cookies directly to the rack. While the cookies are cooling, put the second cookie sheet in the oven and bake in the same way. After you have removed the cookies from the first cookie sheet, line the empty cookie sheet with new parchment paper and bake the rest of the cookies in the same way. Let the cookies cool completely and serve.

Snickerdoodles

Toss a ball of sugar cookie dough in cinnamon and sugar before baking, and voilà, you get a snickerdoodle! Not only do they have a super-funny name, these cookies smell amazing while they bake and taste yummy-licious.

2¾ cups all-purpose flour

1 teaspoon baking powder

¼ teaspoon salt

1 cup (2 sticks) unsalted butter, at room temperature

1¾ cups sugar

2 large eggs

2 teaspoons vanilla extract

1 teaspoon ground cinnamon

 Preheat the oven to 350°F. Line 2 cookie sheets with parchment paper.

In a medium bowl, whisk together the flour, baking powder, and salt. In a large bowl, using an electric mixer, beat the butter and 1½ cups of the sugar on medium speed until well blended, about 1 minute. Add the eggs and vanilla and beat on low speed until combined. Turn off the mixer and scrape down the bowl with a rubber spatula. Add the flour mixture and mix just until blended.

In a small bowl, stir together the remaining ¼ cup sugar and the cinnamon. Scoop up a rounded tablespoonful of dough. Scrape the dough off the spoon into the palm of your hand and roll the dough into a ball. Drop the ball in the cinnamon sugar and roll it around to coat it completely. Place the ball on a prepared cookie sheet. Continue scooping, shaping, and rolling the dough in sugar, spacing the balls about 3 inches apart on the cookie sheets. You should be able to fit 12 cookies on each cookie sheet.

When both cookie sheets are full, bake 1 cookie sheet at a time until the edges of the cookies are lightly browned but the tops are barely colored, 10 to 12 minutes. Ask an adult to help you remove the cookie sheet from the oven and set it on a wire rack. Let cool for 5 minutes, then use a metal spatula to move the cookies directly to the rack. While the cookies are cooling, put the second cookie sheet in the oven and bake in the same way. Repeat to bake the rest of the cookies. Let the cookies cool completely and serve.

Elephant Ears

These swirly cookies are made from puff pastry and become sugary-crisp when baked. They're shaped like puffy elephant ears, which is how these treats get their name.

⋆

2 tablespoons unsalted butter, melted

½ teaspoon vanilla extract

½ cup granulated sugar

½ cup powdered sugar, sifted

1 sheet frozen puff pastry, thawed

Preheat the oven to 375°F. Line 2 cookie sheets with parchment paper. In a small bowl, stir together the melted butter and vanilla; set aside to cool. In another bowl, using a fork, stir together the granulated and powdered sugars. Measure out ½ cup of the sugar mixture and set aside.

Sprinkle 3 tablespoons of the remaining sugar mixture onto a work surface. Place the puff pastry on top of the sugared surface. Sprinkle more of the sugar mixture on top of the pastry, spreading it evenly with your hands.

Using a rolling pin and beginning at the center of the pastry, roll the pastry into a 10-by-20-inch rectangle, sprinkling a little more sugar mixture underneath and on top of the pastry so the pastry doesn't stick.

Using a pastry brush, brush the butter mixture over the surface of the pastry. Sprinkle evenly with the reserved ½ cup sugar mixture. Starting at one short end, fold a 2-inch-wide band of the pastry over onto itself. Repeat this folding until you reach the center of the pastry (probably 3 folds). Now fold the other end of the rectangle in the same way. Fold one band on top of the other to form a long rectangle. Press to stick it together, then ask an adult to help you cut the rectangle crosswise into ½-inch-thick slices. Place the slices on the prepared cookie sheets, spacing them 2 inches apart.

Bake the pastries 1 cookie sheet at a time until golden, about 15 minutes. Let the cookies cool for 5 minutes, then use a metal spatula to move them directly to a wire rack. Let cool completely and serve.

Lemony Cookie Flower Pops

These adorable cookie pops make awesome gifts for your friends or are super sweet to bring to a bake sale. After the cookies are baked, decorate them to look like your favorite flowers, then show off your cookie bouquet.

COOKIES

2⅓ cups all-purpose flour

¼ teaspoon baking powder

⅛ teaspoon salt

1 cup (2 sticks) unsalted butter, at room temperature

⅔ cup granulated sugar

1 large egg

1½ teaspoons vanilla extract

LEMON ICING

1 cup powdered sugar, sifted

1 tablespoon plus 1 teaspoon lemon juice

2 or 3 drops of food coloring in your favorite color(s)

Sprinkles and/or candies for decorating

To make the cookies, in a bowl, whisk together the flour, baking powder, and salt. In a large bowl, using an electric mixer, beat the butter and sugar on medium speed until fluffy and pale, about 5 minutes. Turn off the mixer and scrape down the bowl with a rubber spatula. Add the egg and vanilla and beat until well combined. Add the flour mixture and mix just until blended. Scrape down the bowl. Divide the dough in half and press each piece into a disk. Wrap each disk in plastic wrap and refrigerate until firm, at least 1 hour.

Preheat the oven to 350°F. Line 2 cookie sheets with parchment paper. Sprinkle a work surface with flour. Unwrap 1 chilled dough disk and place it on the floured surface. Using a floured rolling pin, roll out the dough disk into a ¼-inch-thick round. With flower-shaped cookie cutters, cut out as many cookies as possible. Use a metal spatula to transfer the cookies to the prepared cookie sheet, spacing them apart. Press the dough scraps into a disk, wrap in plastic wrap, and refrigerate until firm. Repeat with the second chilled dough disk and the scraps. Insert a wooden ice-pop stick into each cookie flower. Bake the cookies 1 cookie sheet at a time until golden, 15 to 20 minutes. Let the cookies cool for 10 minutes, then use a metal spatula to move them directly to a wire rack. Let cool completely.

To make the icing, in a bowl, whisk together the powdered sugar, lemon juice, and food coloring until smooth. Spread the icing onto the cooled cookies with an icing spatula or use a piping bag to decorate with icing, then decorate with sprinkles while the icing is still wet. Let the icing dry, then serve.

Chocolate Chip Cookie Sandwiches

One of the most scrumptious cookies just got even more irresistible! Take two chocolate chip cookies, put a thick layer of super-chocolaty frosting between them, and you've got a new favorite treat. Don't forget a big glass of cold milk!

2 cups all-purpose flour

1 teaspoon baking soda

½ teaspoon salt

1 cup (2 sticks) unsalted butter, at room temperature

¾ cup firmly packed light brown sugar

¾ cup granulated sugar

2 large eggs

2 teaspoons vanilla extract

2 cups semisweet chocolate chips

Chocolate Frosting (page 64)

 Preheat the oven to 350°F. Line 2 cookie sheets with parchment paper.

In a medium bowl, whisk together the flour, baking soda, and salt. In a large bowl, using an electric mixer, beat the butter, brown sugar, and granulated sugar on medium speed until well blended, about 1 minute. Add the eggs and vanilla and beat on low speed until well combined. Turn off the mixer and scrape down the bowl with a rubber spatula. Add half of the flour mixture and mix on low speed just until blended. Add the rest of the flour mixture and mix just until blended. Add the chocolate chips and beat just until the chips are mixed evenly into the dough. Scrape down the bowl.

Scoop up a rounded tablespoonful of dough, then use your finger to push the dough onto 1 of the prepared cookie sheets. Repeat with the rest of the dough, spacing the mounds 3 inches apart on the cookie sheets.

When both cookie sheets are full, bake 1 cookie sheet at a time until the tops of the cookies are lightly golden in the center, 10 to 12 minutes. Ask an adult to help you remove the cookie sheet from the oven and set it on a wire rack. Let cool for 5 minutes, then use a metal spatula to move the cookies directly to the rack. Repeat to bake the rest of the cookies. Let the cookies cool completely.

Turn half of the cookies bottom side up and spread a thick layer of frosting on the surface of each upside-down cookie. Top each with a second cookie, placing the bottom side onto the filling. Serve right away.

Zesty Lime Cookies

Your kitchen will smell like a tropical beach when you bake these zingy cookies bursting with citrus sunshine. Add green food coloring to the glaze to make it even more lime-tastic.

✩

COOKIES

2½ cups all-purpose flour

½ teaspoon baking powder

¼ teaspoon salt

1 cup (2 sticks) unsalted butter, at room temperature

1 cup granulated sugar

1 large egg

1 tablespoon finely grated lime zest

2 teaspoons vanilla extract

LIME ICING

2 cups powdered sugar, sifted

2 tablespoons lime juice, plus more as needed

1 tablespoon light corn syrup

Colored sugar, for sprinkling (optional)

To make the cookies, in a bowl, whisk together the flour, baking powder, and salt. In a large bowl, using an electric mixer, beat the butter and granulated sugar on medium speed until well blended, about 1 minute. Add the egg, lime zest, and vanilla and beat on low speed until combined. Turn off the mixer and scrape down the bowl with a rubber spatula. Add the flour mixture and mix just until blended. Divide the dough in half, press each piece into a disk, and wrap tightly with plastic wrap. Refrigerate until firm, at least 1 hour.

Preheat the oven to 350°F. Line 2 cookie sheets with parchment paper. Sprinkle a work surface with flour. Unwrap 1 chilled dough disk and place it on the floured surface. Using a floured rolling pin, roll out the disk to a round about ¼ inch thick. With a 2-inch round or fluted cookie cutter, cut out as many cookies as possible. Transfer to the prepared cookie sheets, spacing them 1 inch apart. Press the dough scraps into a disk, wrap in plastic wrap, and refrigerate. Repeat with the second chilled dough disk and the scraps.

Bake the cookies 1 cookie sheet at a time until lightly golden, 10 to 13 minutes. Let the cookies cool for 5 minutes, then use a metal spatula to move them directly to a wire rack. Repeat to bake the rest of the cookies. Let cool completely.

To make the icing, in a bowl, whisk together the powdered sugar, lime juice, and corn syrup until smooth. Using a spoon, drizzle the icing over the cookies, then sprinkle the icing with colored sugar, if you like. Let the icing dry for about 20 minutes and serve.

Chewy Coconut Macaroons

If you're a coconut lover, you'll go crazy for these chewy cookies. Made by beating egg whites into a soft, fluffy mountain, then gently folding them into mounds of shredded coconut, these macaroons are super easy to make and taste extra coconutty.

4 cups sweetened shredded coconut

1 cup sweetened condensed milk

¼ teaspoon salt

2 teaspoons vanilla extract

4 large egg whites

¼ teaspoon cream of tartar

2 tablespoons sugar

 Preheat the oven to 325°F. Line 2 cookie sheets with parchment paper and butter the paper. In a large bowl, using a fork, stir together the coconut, condensed milk, salt, and vanilla until well blended.

In a bowl, combine the egg whites and cream of tartar. Using an electric mixer, beat the egg whites on medium speed until foamy, about 1 minute. Raise the speed to medium-high and continue beating until the egg whites look shiny and smooth and they form peaks that droop when the beaters are lifted (turn off the mixer first!), 2 to 3 minutes. Continue to beat the egg whites while slowly adding the sugar, then keep beating the mixture until it holds stiff peaks when the beaters are lifted (turn off the mixer first!), about 1 minute longer.

Using a rubber spatula, gently mix half of the egg whites into the coconut mixture just until blended, then mix in the rest of the egg whites until no white streaks remain. Scoop rounded tablespoonfuls of the batter onto the prepared cookie sheets, spacing them 1½ inches apart.

Bake the macaroons 1 cookie sheet at a time until the edges and some tips of the coconut shreds are lightly browned, 15 to 17 minutes. Ask an adult to help you remove the cookie sheets from the oven and set them on a wire rack. Let cool for 5 minutes, then use a metal spatula to move the macaroons directly to the rack. Let cool completely and serve.

Sugar Cookies

Sugar cookies are the perfect blank canvas for pretty decorations. Cut the dough into your favorite shapes, and after baking, bedazzle the cookies with icing and sprinkles.

✫

COOKIES

2 cups all-purpose flour

½ teaspoon baking powder

¼ teaspoon salt

½ cup (1 stick) unsalted butter, at room temperature

1 cup granulated sugar

1 large egg

1½ teaspoons vanilla extract

VANILLA ICING

2 cups powdered sugar, sifted

2 tablespoons warm water, plus more as needed

1 tablespoon light corn syrup

1 teaspoon vanilla extract

2 or 3 drops of food coloring in your favorite color(s) (optional)

Colored sugars, sprinkles, and/or candies, for decorating

To make the cookies, in a medium bowl, whisk together the flour, baking powder, and salt. In a large bowl, using an electric mixer, beat the butter and granulated sugar on medium speed until well blended, about 1 minute. Add the egg and vanilla and beat on medium speed until combined. Turn off the mixer and scrape down the bowl with a rubber spatula. Add half of the flour mixture and mix on low speed just until blended. Add the rest of the flour mixture and mix just until blended. The dough will look lumpy, like moist pebbles. Scrape down the bowl.

Dump the dough onto a work surface and press it together into a mound. Divide the dough in half and press each piece into a disk. Wrap each disk tightly in plastic wrap and refrigerate until firm, at least 1 hour or up to overnight.

Preheat the oven to 350°F. Line 2 cookie sheets with parchment paper.

Sprinkle a clean work surface with flour. Unwrap 1 chilled dough disk and place it on the floured surface. Sprinkle the top of the dough with a little more flour. Roll out the dough with a rolling pin until it is about ¼ inch thick. Sprinkle more flour under and over the dough as needed so it doesn't stick. Using your cookie cutters, cut out as many shapes as you can, then use a metal spatula to transfer the cookies to the prepared cookie sheets, spacing them 1 inch apart. Press the dough scraps into a disk, wrap in plastic wrap, and refrigerate until firm. Repeat with the second chilled dough disk and the scraps.

Bake the cookies 1 cookie sheet at a time until the edges of the cookies are lightly browned, 10 to 12 minutes. Ask an adult to help you remove the cookie sheet from the oven and set it on a wire rack. Let cool for 10 minutes, then use a metal spatula to move the cookies directly to the rack. Let cool completely. If there is remaining dough, repeat to bake the rest of the cookies.

To make the icing, in a medium bowl, whisk together the powdered sugar, water, corn syrup, and vanilla until smooth. Add the food coloring (if using) and whisk to combine. If you're using more than 1 color, divide the icing among small bowls and make each one a different color by whisking a couple drops of food coloring into each bowl.

To decorate the cookies, using an icing spatula or a butter knife, spread icing on each cookie. While the icing is soft, decorate the cookies with colored sugars, candies, or sprinkles. Let the icing dry for about 20 minutes and serve.

Chocolate Crinkle Cookies

Coated in a flurry of powdered sugar and extra-fudgy inside, these cool-looking cookies will satisfy even the biggest chocolate craving. These treats also go by the name "earthquake cookies" because of their crackly tops.

½ cup powdered sugar, sifted

1⅔ cups all-purpose flour

½ cup unsweetened cocoa powder, sifted

1½ teaspoons baking powder

¼ teaspoon salt

½ cup (1 stick) unsalted butter, at room temperature

1¼ cups granulated sugar

2 large eggs

½ teaspoon vanilla extract

 Preheat the oven to 350°F. Line 2 cookie sheets with parchment paper. Put the powdered sugar into a medium bowl and set aside.

In another medium bowl, whisk together the flour, cocoa, baking powder, and salt. In a large bowl, using an electric mixer, beat the butter and granulated sugar on medium speed until fluffy and pale, about 3 minutes. Turn off the mixer and scrape down the bowl with a rubber spatula. Add 1 egg and beat on medium speed until blended. Add the other egg and the vanilla and beat until blended. Turn off the mixer and add the flour mixture. Mix on low speed just until blended. Scrape down the bowl.

Scoop up a rounded tablespoonful of dough. Scrape the dough off the spoon into the palm of your hand. Roll the dough into a ball, set it on a large plate, and shape the rest of the dough into balls in the same way.

When all of the dough has been shaped, roll the balls in the powdered sugar until completely covered. Place the balls on the prepared cookie sheets, spacing them about 2 inches apart.

Bake the cookies 1 cookie sheet at a time until crackled and puffed, 10 to 12 minutes. Ask an adult to help you remove the cookie sheet from the oven and set it on a wire rack. Let cool for 15 minutes, then use a metal spatula to move the cookies directly to the rack. Let cool completely and serve.

Double choco-rific
Make these brownie-like cookies even more chocolaty by adding ½ cup mini chocolate chips to the batter.

Ice Cream Sandwiches

What's more delicious than a bowlful of your favorite ice cream? A big, melty scoop smashed between two crispy-chewy chocolate cookies! Freeze an extra batch of the baked cookies in an airtight container so they're ready to serve anytime.

1 cup semisweet chocolate chips

½ cup (1 stick) unsalted butter

¼ cup light corn syrup

1 cup all-purpose flour

½ teaspoon baking soda

¼ teaspoon salt

⅓ cup sugar

1 large egg

1 teaspoon vanilla extract

Sprinkles, small candies, chopped toasted nuts, mini chocolate chips, or crushed cookies, for decorating

1 quart ice cream (your favorite flavor), softened for 10–15 minutes at room temperature

Position 2 racks in the upper third of the oven so that they are evenly spaced and preheat the oven to 350°F. Line 2 cookie sheets with parchment paper.

In a saucepan, combine the chocolate chips, butter, and corn syrup. Ask an adult to help you place the pan over medium-low heat. Warm the mixture until the butter melts. Don't let the chocolate get too hot! Remove the pan from the heat and stir the chocolate mixture with a rubber spatula until it is melted and smooth. Using the rubber spatula, scrape the mixture into a large bowl and let cool. In another bowl, whisk together the flour, baking soda, and salt.

Add the sugar to the cooled chocolate mixture and stir well with a wooden spoon. Stir in the egg and vanilla until blended. Scrape down the bowl with the rubber spatula. Add the flour mixture to the chocolate mixture and stir with a wooden spoon until blended.

Scoop up a rounded tablespoonful of dough, then use your finger to push the dough onto 1 of the prepared cookie sheets. Repeat with the rest of the dough, spacing the mounds 4 inches apart on the cookie sheets. You should be able to fit 9 cookies on each cookie sheet. With your fingers, pat the mounds of dough to form 2-inch rounds so that they will spread into neat circles.

When both cookie sheets are full, bake the cookies until they puff and then begin to sink, 10 to 12 minutes. Don't overbake them, or they will become too crunchy. Ask an adult to help you remove the cookie sheets from the oven and set them on wire racks. Let cool for 15 minutes, then use a metal spatula to move the cookies directly to the racks. Let cool completely. Repeat to bake the rest of the dough.

Put the sprinkles and/or other decorations into small bowls. Turn half of the cookies bottom side up and top each with a scoop of ice cream. Place a second cookie flat side down on top of the ice cream. One at a time, pick up the ice cream sandwiches and gently press the cookies together to squish the ice cream all the way to the edges. Use a butter knife to smooth the edges, if needed. Working quickly, roll the ice cream edges in the decorations until coated all around.

Wrap each ice cream sandwich in plastic wrap and freeze until firm, at least 2 hours. Serve frozen with lots of napkins.

Madeleines

Orange Madeleines

A little freshly grated orange zest gives these adorable shell-shaped mini cakes an amazing aroma and lots of flair. The zest adds pretty orange flecks to the cakes, too.

⭐

5 tablespoons unsalted butter, melted and cooled

½ cup cake flour, plus more for dusting the pan

½ teaspoon baking powder

1 large egg

¼ cup sugar

2 teaspoons finely grated orange zest

Position a rack in the lower third of the oven and preheat the oven to 400°F. Using a pastry brush and 1 tablespoon of the butter, coat the 12 molds of a madeleine pan with a thick layer of butter, making sure you coat each and every ridge. Dust the molds with flour, tilting the pan to coat all of the surfaces. Turn the pan upside down over the kitchen sink and tap it gently to knock out the excess flour.

Sift together the flour and baking powder into a bowl. In another bowl, using an electric mixer, beat together the egg and sugar on medium speed for 30 seconds. Increase the speed to high and beat until very thick and quadrupled in bulk, about 10 minutes. Beat in the orange zest. Turn off the mixer. Sprinkle the flour mixture over the egg mixture. Using a rubber spatula, gently fold in the flour mixture, then fold in the remaining 4 tablespoons butter.

Scoop a heaping tablespoonful of batter into each mold. The molds should be three-fourths full. Bake until the cookies are golden brown at the edges and the tops spring back when lightly touched (ask an adult for help!), 10 to 12 minutes. Ask an adult to help you remove the pan from the oven, invert it onto a wire rack right away, and tap the pan on the rack to release the madeleines. If any of the cookies stick, use a butter knife to loosen the edges, being careful not to touch the hot pan, and invert and tap again. Serve slightly warm. These are best eaten the same day they are baked.

Chocolate-Dipped Vanilla Madeleines

Sweet and fancy French madeleines are très cute when dipped into rich melted chocolate. Serve these at your next tea party. Bon appétit!

5 tablespoons unsalted butter, melted and cooled

½ cup cake flour, plus more for dusting the pan

½ teaspoon baking powder

1 large egg

¼ cup sugar

1 teaspoon vanilla extract

⅓ cup semisweet chocolate chips

Position a rack in the lower third of the oven and preheat the oven to 400°F. Using a pastry brush and 1 tablespoon of the butter, coat the 12 molds of a madeleine pan with a thick layer of butter, making sure you coat each and every ridge. Dust the molds with flour, tilting the pan to coat all of the surfaces. Turn the pan upside down over the kitchen sink and tap it gently to knock out the excess flour.

Sift together the flour and baking powder into a bowl. In another bowl, using an electric mixer, beat together the egg and sugar on medium speed for 30 seconds. Increase the speed to high and beat until very thick and quadrupled in bulk, about 10 minutes. Beat in the vanilla. Turn off the mixer. Sprinkle the flour mixture over the egg mixture. Using a rubber spatula, gently fold in the flour mixture, then fold in the remaining 4 tablespoons butter.

Scoop a heaping tablespoonful of batter into each mold. The molds should be three-fourths full. Bake until the cookies are golden brown at the edges and the tops spring back when lightly touched (ask an adult for help!), 10 to 12 minutes. Ask an adult to help you remove the pan from the oven, invert it onto a wire rack right away, and tap the pan on the rack to release the madeleines. If any of the cookies stick, use a butter knife to loosen the edges, being careful not to touch the hot pan, and invert and tap again. Let cool while you melt the chocolate for dipping.

To dip the madeleines in chocolate, line a cookie sheet with parchment paper. Place the chocolate chips in a small microwave-safe bowl. Ask an adult to help you microwave the chocolate on high heat, stirring every 20 seconds, until it's melted and smooth. Don't let the chocolate get too hot! One at a time, carefully dip the wide, rounded end of each madeleine into the chocolate, then set it, shell-side up, on the prepared cookie sheet.

Refrigerate the cookies until the chocolate is set, 10 to 15 minutes. Serve. These are best eaten the same day they are baked.

A pretty gift
Chocolate-dipped madeleines are a special treat and make a memorable present for someone sweet.

Tea perfect!
These sweet little cakes are ideal for an afternoon tea party. Serve them with fresh berries and fruity herbal tea.

Honey Madeleines

These buttery, honey-licious cakes are surprisingly easy to make. You need only a few ingredients, an electric mixer, and a shell-shaped mold. And with a little imagination, you'll feel like you're in a bakery in Paris!

5 tablespoons unsalted butter, melted and cooled

½ cup cake flour, plus more for dusting the pan

½ teaspoon baking powder

1 large egg

3 tablespoons sugar

2 tablespoons honey

2 teaspoons orange flower water

 Position a rack in the lower third of the oven and preheat the oven to 400°F. Using a pastry brush and 1 tablespoon of the butter, coat the 12 molds of a madeleine pan with a thick layer of butter, making sure you coat each and every ridge. Dust the molds with flour, tilting the pan to coat all of the surfaces. Turn the pan upside down over the kitchen sink and tap it gently to knock out the excess flour.

Sift together the flour and baking powder into a bowl. In another bowl, using an electric mixer, beat together the egg and sugar on medium speed for 30 seconds. Increase the speed to high and beat until very thick and quadrupled in bulk, about 10 minutes. Add the honey and orange flower water and beat until combined. Turn off the mixer. Sprinkle the flour mixture over the egg mixture. Using a rubber spatula, gently fold in the flour mixture, then fold in the remaining 4 tablespoons butter.

Scoop a heaping tablespoonful of batter into each mold. The molds should be three-fourths full. Bake until the cookies are golden brown at the edges and the tops spring back when lightly touched (ask an adult for help!), 10 to 12 minutes. Ask an adult to help you remove the pan from the oven, invert it onto a wire rack right away, and tap the pan on the rack to release the madeleines. If any of the cookies stick, use a butter knife to loosen the edges, being careful not to touch the hot pan, and invert and tap again. Serve slightly warm. These are best eaten the same day they are baked.

Chocolate Madeleines

These scrumptious little chocolate cakes are perfect for baking with your friends. To make them super-duper choco-rific, dip the madeleines in melted chocolate chips following the directions on page 53.

5 tablespoons unsalted butter, melted and cooled

¼ cup all-purpose flour, plus more for dusting the pan

¼ cup unsweetened cocoa powder

½ teaspoon baking powder

⅛ teaspoon salt

1 large egg

6 tablespoons sugar

½ teaspoon vanilla extract

Confectioners' (powdered) sugar for dusting

Position a rack in the lower third of the oven and preheat the oven to 375°F. Using a pastry brush and 1 tablespoon of the butter, coat the 12 molds of a madeleine pan with a thick layer of butter, making sure you coat each and every ridge. Dust the molds with flour, tilting the pan to coat all of the surfaces. Turn the pan upside down over the kitchen sink and tap it gently to knock out the excess flour.

Sift together the flour, cocoa powder, baking powder, and salt into a bowl. In another bowl, using an electric mixer, beat together the egg and sugar on medium speed for 30 seconds. Increase the speed to high and beat until very thick and quadrupled in bulk, about 10 minutes. Beat in the vanilla. Turn off the mixer. Sprinkle the flour mixture over the egg mixture. Using a rubber spatula, gently fold in the flour mixture, then fold in the remaining 4 tablespoons butter.

Scoop a heaping tablespoonful of batter into each mold. The molds should be three-fourths full. Bake until the edges are set and the tops spring back when lightly touched (ask an adult for help!), 10 to 12 minutes. Ask an adult to help you remove the pan from the oven, invert it onto a wire rack right away, and tap the pan on the rack to release the madeleines. If any of the cookies stick, use a butter knife to loosen the edges, being careful not to touch the hot pan, and invert and tap again. Use a fine-mesh sieve or a sifter, dust them with confectioners' sugar. Serve slightly warm. These are best eaten the same day they are baked.

Cupcakes

Pumpkin Cupcakes

Thick, tangy cream cheese frosting is the perfect topping for these delicious spiced cupcakes. Surprise your family and serve them for a winter holiday or bake them for a special autumn birthday party.

1½ cups all-purpose flour

2 teaspoons baking powder

½ teaspoon baking soda

2 teaspoons ground cinnamon

1 teaspoon ground ginger

¼ teaspoon ground nutmeg

¼ teaspoon salt

½ cup (1 stick) unsalted butter, at room temperature

⅔ cup firmly packed light brown sugar

2 large eggs

½ cup canned pumpkin puree

½ cup sour cream

Cream Cheese Frosting (page 76)

 Preheat the oven to 350°F. Line a standard 12-cup muffin pan with paper or foil liners.

In a medium bowl, whisk together the flour, baking powder, baking soda, cinnamon, ginger, nutmeg, and salt. In a large bowl, using an electric mixer, beat the butter and brown sugar on medium-high speed until fluffy, about 3 minutes. Add the eggs one at a time, beating well after adding each one. Turn off the mixer and scrape down the bowl with a rubber spatula. Add the pumpkin puree and sour cream and mix with the rubber spatula until blended. Add the flour mixture and stir with the rubber spatula just until blended. The batter will be thick.

Divide the batter evenly among the muffin cups, filling them nearly full. Bake until a wooden skewer inserted into the center of a cupcake comes out clean (ask an adult for help!), about 18 minutes. Ask an adult to help you remove the pan from the oven and set it on a wire rack. Let the cupcakes cool in the pan for 10 minutes, then lift them out and set them directly on the rack. Let cool completely.

Using a small icing spatula or a butter knife (or a piping bag), frost the cupcakes and serve.

Devil's Food Cupcakes

Despite their name, these cupcakes are anything but devilish. Moist chocolate cake and rich chocolate frosting—decorated with plenty of rainbow sprinkles or other candies—are just heavenly good!

CUPCAKES

1 cup all-purpose flour

¼ cup unsweetened cocoa powder

1 teaspoon baking soda

¼ teaspoon salt

⅓ cup granulated sugar

⅓ cup firmly packed light brown sugar

4 tablespoons (½ stick) unsalted butter, at room temperature

1 large egg

1 teaspoon vanilla extract

¾ cup buttermilk

CHOCOLATE FROSTING

3½ cups powdered sugar

1 cup cocoa powder

½ cup (1 stick) unsalted butter, at room temperature

1 teaspoon vanilla extract

1 cup heavy cream

 Preheat the oven to 350°F. Line a standard 12-cup muffin pan.

To make the cupcakes, in a bowl, whisk together the flour, cocoa, baking soda, and salt. In a large bowl, using an electric mixer, beat the granulated sugar, brown sugar, and butter on medium-high speed until fluffy, about 3 minutes. Add the egg and vanilla and beat until combined. Turn off the mixer and scrape down the bowl with a rubber spatula. Add half of the flour mixture and mix on low speed just until blended. Turn off the mixer. Pour in the buttermilk and mix on low speed just until combined. Turn off the mixer. Add the rest of the flour mixture and mix just until blended. Scrape down the bowl.

Divide the batter evenly among the prepared muffin cups, filling each about three-fourths full. Bake until a wooden skewer inserted into the center of a cupcake comes out clean (ask an adult for help!), 18 to 20 minutes. Ask an adult to help you remove the pan from the oven and set it on a wire rack. Let the cupcakes cool for 10 minutes, then transfer them to the rack. Let cool.

To make the frosting, sift together the powdered sugar and cocoa into a bowl. Add the butter. Using an electric mixer, beat the mixture on low speed until crumbly. Add the vanilla and beat until combined. Turn off the mixer. Add the cream and beat until the frosting is smooth, about 1 minute. If the frosting is too thick, add more of the cream until it becomes smooth and spreadable.

Frost the cupcakes. Decorate with sprinkles or candies, if you like, and serve.

White Chocolate & Raspberry Cupcakes

These sweet, berry-licious cupcakes are decorated with powdered sugar, not frosting, so they're perfect for taking on a picnic or packing in a lunchbox. If you like, you can stir in chopped strawberries or blackberries instead of raspberries.

✫

1¼ cups all-purpose flour

1½ teaspoon baking powder

⅛ teaspoon salt

⅔ cup granulated sugar

4 tablespoons (½ stick) unsalted butter, at room temperature

1 large egg

1 teaspoon vanilla extract

½ cup whole milk

½ cup white chocolate chips

1 cup raspberries, halved if large

Powdered sugar, for dusting

 Preheat the oven to 350°F. Line a standard 12-cup muffin pan.

In a medium bowl, whisk together the flour, baking powder, and salt. In a large bowl, using an electric mixer, beat the granulated sugar and butter on medium-high speed until fluffy and pale, about 3 minutes. Add the egg and vanilla and beat until combined. Turn off the mixer and scrape down the bowl with a rubber spatula. Add half of the flour mixture and mix on low speed just until blended. Turn off the mixer. Pour in the milk and mix on low speed just until combined. Turn off the mixer. Add the rest of the flour mixture and mix just until blended. Turn off the mixer. Add the white chocolate chips and stir gently with the rubber spatula, then add the raspberries and stir gently just until combined.

Divide the batter evenly among the prepared muffin cups, filling each about three-fourths full. Bake until lightly golden and a wooden skewer inserted into the center of a cupcake comes out clean (ask an adult for help!), 18 to 20 minutes. Ask an adult to help you remove the pan from the oven and set it on a wire rack. Let the cupcakes cool in the pan for 10 minutes, then lift them out and set them directly on the rack. Let cool completely.

Put the powdered sugar in a fine-mesh sieve and dust the cupcakes with sugar. Serve right away.

Sweet Lemony Cupcakes

These cupcakes are sweet, tart, and perfect for enjoying in the summer sunshine. Bake up a batch or two to sell at your lemonade stand and you'll have customers coming back for more!

CUPCAKES

2¼ cups all-purpose flour

1½ teaspoons baking powder

¾ teaspoon salt

5 teaspoons poppy seeds

¾ cup (1½ sticks) unsalted butter, at room temperature

1½ cups granulated sugar

2 teaspoons finely grated lemon zest

2 large eggs

¾ cup whole milk

GLAZE

2 cups powdered sugar, sifted

3 tablespoons lemon juice

Yellow decorating sugar or white and yellow sprinkles, for decorating

 Preheat the oven to 325°F. Line 2 standard 12-cup muffin pans.

To make the cupcakes, in a bowl, whisk together the flour, baking powder, salt, and poppy seeds. In a large bowl, using an electric mixer, beat the butter, granulated sugar, and lemon zest on medium-high speed until fluffy and pale, about 3 minutes. Add the eggs one at a time, beating well after adding each one. Turn off the mixer and scrape down the bowl with a rubber spatula. Add half of the flour mixture and mix on low speed just until blended. Turn off the mixer. Pour in the milk and mix on low speed until combined. Turn off the mixer. Add the rest of the flour mixture and mix just until blended. Turn off the mixer and scrape down the bowl.

Divide the batter evenly among the muffin cups, filling each three-fourths full. Bake until golden brown and a wooden skewer inserted into the center of a cupcake comes out clean (ask an adult for help!), 18 to 20 minutes. Ask an adult to help you remove the pans from the oven and set them on wire racks. Let the cupcakes cool for 10 minutes, then transfer them to the racks. Let cool.

To make the icing, in a bowl, whisk together the powdered sugar and lemon juice. Spoon some icing on top of each cooled cupcake and use the back of the spoon to spread it to the edge. Let the icing stand for a minute, until it smooths out. While the icing is soft, sprinkle the cupcakes with the sugar or sprinkles. Don't wait too long or the icing will harden and the decorations won't stick! Let the icing dry for about 20 minutes and serve.

Red Velvet Cupcakes

These red velvet cupcakes have just a hint of cocoa and get their jewel-like red color from a little food coloring. Piled high with cream cheese frosting, these festive treats are ready for a party!

2 tablespoons unsweetened cocoa powder, sifted

⅓ cup boiling water

1 cup buttermilk

12 tablespoons (1½ sticks) unsalted butter, at room temperature

1½ cups sugar

3 large eggs

2 to 3 teaspoons red food coloring

2 teaspoons vanilla extract

¼ teaspoon salt

2½ cups all-purpose flour

1½ teaspoons baking soda

1 teaspoon white vinegar

Cream Cheese Frosting (page 76)

 Preheat the oven to 350°F. Line 18 cups (of two 12-cup muffin pans).

In a heatproof bowl, whisk together the cocoa and the boiling water, then whisk in the buttermilk. In a large bowl, using an electric mixer, beat the butter and sugar on medium-high speed until fluffy and pale, about 3 minutes. Add the eggs one at a time, beating well after adding each one. Add the food coloring, vanilla, and salt and beat until combined. Turn off the mixer and scrape down the bowl with a rubber spatula. Add half of the flour and beat on low speed just until blended. Turn off the mixer. Pour in the buttermilk mixture and mix on low speed just until blended. Turn off the mixer. Add the remaining flour and mix just until blended. Turn off the mixer one last time and scrape down the bowl. In a small bowl, stir together the baking soda and vinegar, then quickly stir the mixture into the batter with the rubber spatula.

Divide the batter among the prepared muffin cups, filling them about three-fourths full. Put the pans in the oven and bake until a wooden skewer inserted into the center of a cupcake comes out clean (ask an adult for help!), about 18 minutes. Ask an adult to help you remove the pans from the oven and set them on wire racks. Let the cupcakes cool in the pans for 10 minutes, then transfer them to the racks. Let cool completely.

Using a small icing spatula or a butter knife (or a piping bag), frost the cupcakes and serve.

Strawberry Cheesecake Cupcakes

Swirled with sticky strawberry jam, these pretty little cheesecakes are baked in a muffin pan just like cupcakes! Try different flavors of jam, like raspberry or cherry, to mix it up.

CRUST

6 graham crackers, broken into pieces

2 teaspoons sugar

3 tablespoons unsalted butter, melted

Pinch of salt

FILLING

½ cup strawberry jam

2 (8-ounce) packages cream cheese, at room temperature

⅔ cup sugar

¼ cup sour cream

1 teaspoon vanilla extract

2 large eggs

1 tablespoon all-purpose flour

 Preheat the oven to 325°F. Line 16 cups (of two 12-cup muffin pans).

To make the crust, in the bowl of a food processor, process the graham crackers to fine crumbs. Pour the crumbs into a bowl (you should have ⅔ cup). Add the sugar, melted butter, and salt and, using a fork, stir until the crumbs are evenly moistened. Divide the mixture evenly among the prepared muffin cups (about 1 tablespoon per cup). Press the crumbs into the bottom of each cup. Bake until lightly golden, about 4 minutes. Ask an adult to help you remove the pans from the oven and set them on wire racks.

To make the filling, in the clean food processor bowl, process the jam until smooth. If the jam is very thick, add a little lemon juice or water to thin it until it is like a sauce. Scrape into a bowl and set aside. Clean the processor bowl.

In the food processor, process the cream cheese until smooth, about 3 minutes. Add the sugar and process until smooth, about 30 seconds. Scrape down the bowl. Add the sour cream and vanilla and process until combined. Add the eggs, one at a time, processing well after adding each one. Add the flour and process until combined. Scrape down the bowl and process once more.

Divide the filling evenly among the prepared muffin cups, filling each three-fourths full. Top each with a small amount of the jam, then use a toothpick to swirl the mixtures together, creating a marbled look. Bake until the cheesecakes puff and are set, about 23 minutes. Ask an adult to help you remove the pans, then let cool completely in the pans. Cover with plastic wrap and refrigerate until chilled, at least 3 hours or up to overnight. Serve.

Carrot Cupcakes with Cream Cheese Frosting

Is there a better way to eat your veggies than tucked into an amazing cupcake that's topped off with ooey gooey cream cheese frosting? These are veggie-rific!

CUPCAKES

2¼ cups all-purpose flour

1 cup brown sugar

1 tablespoon baking powder

1 teaspoon cinnamon

½ teaspoon salt

1½ cups peeled and grated carrots

¾ cup vegetable oil

4 large eggs

1½ teaspoons vanilla extract

CREAM CHEESE FROSTING

1 (8-ounce) package cream cheese, at room temperature

4 tablespoons (½ stick) unsalted butter, at room temperature

2 teaspoons vanilla extract

1 cup powdered sugar

 Preheat the oven to 325°F. Line 18 cups (of two 12-cup muffin pans) with paper or foil liners.

To make the cupcakes, in a large bowl, whisk together the flour, brown sugar, baking powder, cinnamon, and salt. In a small bowl, combine the carrots, oil, eggs, and vanilla and whisk until blended. Add the carrot mixture to the flour mixture and stir with a rubber spatula just until blended.

Divide the batter evenly among the prepared muffin cups. Put the pans in the oven and bake until a wooden skewer inserted into the center of a cupcake comes out clean (ask an adult for help!), 16 to 18 minutes. Ask an adult to help you remove the pans from the oven and set them on wire racks. Let the cupcakes cool in the pans for 10 minutes, then lift them out and set them directly on the racks. Let cool completely.

To make the frosting, in a bowl, using an electric mixer, beat the cream cheese, butter, and vanilla on medium-high speed until light and fluffy, about 2 minutes. Turn off the mixer. Sift the powdered sugar through a fine-mesh sieve, ½ cup at a time, over the cream cheese mixture, then beat well after each addition. Turn off the mixer and scrape down the bowl with a rubber spatula. The frosting should be spreadable. If it's too soft, refrigerate it for about 15 minutes.

Using a small icing spatula or a butter knife, frost the cupcakes and serve.

PB & J Cupcakes

Inspired by peanut butter and jelly sandwiches, these jam-filled vanilla cupcakes are topped with peanut butter frosting. Add one to your lunchbox for a sweet treat!

CUPCAKES

1¼ cups all-purpose flour

1¼ teaspoons baking powder

¼ teaspoon salt

¾ cup granulated sugar

6 tablespoons (¾ stick) unsalted butter, at room temperature

2 large eggs

1 teaspoon vanilla extract

⅓ cup whole milk

PB FROSTING

6 tablespoons (¾ stick) unsalted butter, at room temperature

¾ cup smooth peanut butter

¾ cup powdered sugar, sifted

¼ cup heavy cream

¾ cup fruit jam or preserves

 Preheat the oven to 350°F. Line a standard 12-cup muffin pan.

To make the cupcakes, in a bowl, whisk together the flour, baking powder, and salt. In another bowl, using an electric mixer, beat the granulated sugar and butter on medium-high speed until fluffy and pale, about 3 minutes. Add the eggs and vanilla and beat until combined. Turn off the mixer and scrape down the bowl with a rubber spatula. Add half of the flour mixture and mix on low speed just until blended. Turn off the mixer. Pour in the milk and mix on low speed just until combined. Turn off the mixer. Add the rest of the flour mixture and mix just until blended. Scrape down the bowl.

Divide the batter evenly among the prepared muffin cups, filling each about three-fourths full. Bake until lightly golden and a wooden skewer inserted into the center of a cupcake comes out clean (ask an adult for help!), 18 to 20 minutes. Ask an adult to help you remove the pan from the oven and set it on a wire rack. Let the cupcakes cool in the pan for 10 minutes, then transfer them to the rack. Let cool completely.

To make the frosting, in a bowl, using an electric mixer, beat the butter, peanut butter, powdered sugar, and cream on medium-low speed until smooth and combined, about 2 minutes. Ask an adult to help you use a serrated knife and halve each cupcake horizontally. Spread about 1 tablespoon of jam on each cupcake bottom, then replace the tops. Using a small icing spatula or a butter knife, frost the cupcakes and serve.

S'mores Cupcakes

No campfire? No problem! Here's a way to turn everyone's favorite camping treat into delicious oven-baked goodies. These rich chocolate cupcakes are loaded with mini marshmallows and crumbled graham crackers. Yum!

1 cup all-purpose flour

¼ cup unsweetened cocoa powder, sifted

¾ teaspoon baking soda

¼ teaspoon salt

6 tablespoons (¾ stick) unsalted butter, at room temperature

½ cup granulated sugar

⅓ cup firmly packed light brown sugar

1 large egg

1 teaspoon vanilla extract

¾ cup buttermilk

⅔ cup roughly crumbled graham crackers (about 3 crackers), plus more for decorating

⅓ cup mini marshmallows, plus more for decorating

⅔ cup semisweet chocolate chips

 Preheat the oven to 350°F. Line 18 cups (of two 12-cup muffin pans).

In a medium bowl, whisk together the flour, cocoa, baking soda, and salt. In another bowl, using an electric mixer, beat the butter and sugars on medium-high speed until fluffy and pale, about 3 minutes. Add the egg and vanilla and beat until combined. Turn off the mixer and scrape down the bowl with a rubber spatula. Add half of the flour mixture and mix on low speed just until blended. Turn off the mixer. Pour in the buttermilk and mix on low speed just until combined. Turn off the mixer. Add the rest of the flour mixture and mix just until blended. Turn off the mixer. Using a rubber spatula, stir in the graham crackers and marshmallows.

Divide the batter evenly among the prepared muffin cups, filling each about two-thirds full. Bake until a wooden skewer inserted into the center of a cupcake comes out clean (ask an adult for help!), 18 to 20 minutes. Ask an adult to help you remove the pans from the oven and set them on wire racks. Let the cupcakes cool for 10 minutes, then transfer them to the racks. Let cool.

Place the chocolate chips in a small microwave-safe bowl. Ask an adult to help you microwave the chocolate on high heat, stirring every 20 seconds, until it's melted and smooth. Don't let the chocolate get too hot!

Spread a thin layer of melted chocolate on each cupcake, then top with graham crackers and marshmallows. Let the chocolate set, then serve.

Black Bottom Cupcakes

There's a lot to love about these cupcakes: super chocolaty cake on the outside, creamy cheesecake on the inside, and melty chocolate chips on top. Try using a zippered plastic bag as a piping bag to fill the center of each cupcake before baking to keep things tidy.

FILLING

1 (8-ounce) package cream cheese, at room temperature

½ cup sugar

1 large egg

CUPCAKES

1½ cups cold water

½ cup vegetable oil

2 teaspoons vanilla extract

3 teaspoons balsamic vinegar

2⅓ cups all-purpose flour

½ cup unsweetened cocoa powder, sifted

1 teaspoon baking soda

1 cup sugar

½ teaspoon salt

½ cup semisweet chocolate chips

 Preheat the oven to 350°F. Line 2 standard 12-cup muffin pans with paper or foil liners.

To make the filling, in a medium bowl, using an electric mixer, beat the cream cheese, sugar, and egg on medium speed until smooth, about 2 minutes.

To make the cupcakes, in a medium bowl, combine the water, oil, vanilla, and balsamic vinegar. In a large bowl, whisk together the flour, cocoa, baking soda, sugar, and salt. Pour the wet ingredients into the flour mixture and stir with a wooden spoon until the batter is smooth (it will be runny).

Fill the muffin cups three-fourths full. Using a tablespoon measure, spoon about 1 tablespoon of the filling into the center of the batter. You will see the chocolate batter rise as the filling fills the middle. Fill all of the cupcakes.

Sprinkle the cupcakes with the chocolate chips, dividing them evenly. Put the pans in the oven and bake until a wooden skewer inserted into the center of a cupcake comes out clean (ask an adult for help!), about 25 minutes. Ask an adult to help you remove the pans from the oven and set them on wire racks. Let the cupcakes cool in the pans for 10 minutes, then lift them out and set them directly on the racks. Let cool completely and serve.

Line with color
Add personality and pizzazz to your cupcakes by using an array of liners in different colors and fun patterns.

Snowball Cupcakes

These tender vanilla treats are covered in shredded coconut, so they look like fluffy snowballs—but they taste way yummier! You can color the frosting and the coconut by mixing a few drops of food coloring into each before decorating the cupcakes.

2¾ cups all-purpose flour

2 tablespoons cornstarch

1 tablespoon baking powder

⅛ teaspoon salt

1½ cups sugar

¾ cup (1½ sticks) unsalted butter, at room temperature

3 large eggs

¾ cup whole milk

½ cup water

1 tablespoon vanilla extract

Cream Cheese Frosting (page 76)

2 cups shredded sweetened coconut

 Preheat the oven to 350°F. Line two standard 12-cup muffin pans with paper or foil liners.

In a medium bowl, whisk together the flour, cornstarch, baking powder, and salt. In a large bowl, using an electric mixer, beat the sugar and the butter on medium-high speed until fluffy and pale, about 3 minutes. Add the eggs, one at a time, beating well after adding each one. Turn off the mixer and scrape down the bowl with a rubber spatula. Add the milk, water, and vanilla and beat until combined. Turn off the mixer and scrape down the bowl. Add half of the flour mixture and mix on low speed just until blended. Turn off the mixer. Add the rest of the flour mixture and mix just until blended. Scrape down the bowl.

Divide the batter evenly among the prepared muffin cups, filling them about two-thirds full. Put the pans in the oven and bake until a toothpick inserted into the center of a cupcake comes out clean (ask an adult for help!), 18 to 20 minutes. Ask an adult to help you remove the pans from the oven and set them on wire racks. Let the cupcakes cool in the pans for 10 minutes, then lift them out and set them directly on the racks. Let cool completely.

Using a small icing spatula or a butter knife, frost the cupcakes. Sprinkle them with the shredded coconut and serve.

More Treats

Chocolate-Peanut Butter Brownies

A big pan of fudgy brownies is one of the best things to share with your friends. Creamy pools of peanut butter make these an even more delicious treats!

¾ cup (1½ sticks) unsalted butter

8 ounces semisweet chocolate, chopped into small pieces

4 large eggs

1 cup sugar

1 teaspoon vanilla extract

¼ teaspoon salt

1 cup all-purpose flour

8 tablespoons smooth peanut butter

¾ cup semisweet chocolate chips

 Preheat the oven to 350°F. Line a 9-inch square baking pan with parchment paper, extending it up and over the sides on 2 sides.

Select a saucepan and a heatproof bowl that fits snugly on top of the pan. Fill the pan one-third full of water, making sure the water doesn't touch the bottom of the bowl. Ask an adult to help you place the saucepan over medium heat. When the water is steaming, place the bowl on top of the saucepan and add the butter and chocolate to the bowl. Heat, stirring with a rubber spatula, until the mixture is melted and smooth, about 5 minutes. Don't let the chocolate get too hot! Ask an adult to help you remove the bowl from the saucepan (the bowl will be hot!) and set aside to cool slightly.

In a bowl, using an electric mixer, beat the eggs on medium speed until pale, about 4 minutes. Add the sugar, vanilla, and salt and beat until well combined. Turn off the mixer. Add the chocolate mixture and beat until blended. Turn off the mixer and scrape down the bowl with a rubber spatula. Stir in the flour with the rubber spatula just until blended.

Scrape the batter into the pan and smooth the top. Using a tablespoon measure, drop 8 dollops of peanut butter over the top, spacing them evenly. Sprinkle with the chocolate chips. Bake until a toothpick inserted into the center comes out clean (ask an adult for help!), 25 to 30 minutes. Ask an adult to help you remove the pan from the oven and put it on a wire rack. Let cool completely, then use the edges of the parchment paper to lift the brownie "cake" from the pan. Place on a cutting board and cut into 16 squares and serve.

Strawberry Shortcakes

Strawberry shortcakes are great for a party. Set out a plateful of tender shortcakes and bowls of sliced strawberries and whipped cream, and invite your friends to put together their own "berry" delicious desserts!

SHORTCAKES

2 cups all-purpose flour

¼ cup granulated sugar

2 teaspoons baking powder

¼ teaspoon salt

6 tablespoons (¾ stick) cold unsalted butter, cut into small cubes

¾ cup heavy cream

STRAWBERRIES

1 pound fresh strawberries

1 to 2 tablespoons granulated sugar

WHIPPED CREAM

1 cup cold heavy cream

1 tablespoon granulated sugar

1 teaspoon vanilla extract

Powdered sugar, for serving

 To make the shortcakes, preheat the oven to 375°F. Line a cookie sheet with a piece of parchment paper.

In a large bowl, whisk together the flour, granulated sugar, baking powder, and salt until evenly blended. Add the butter cubes. Using a pastry blender or 2 butter knives, cut the butter into the dry ingredients until the mixture looks like coarse crumbs, with some chunks the size of peas. Pour in the cream and stir with a wooden spoon until the dough starts to come together.

Sprinkle a work surface with flour. Turn the dough out of the bowl and onto the floured surface and pat it into a disk. Roll it out with a rolling pin, giving the disk a quarter turn now and then, into a round slab that's 1 inch thick. Pat the sides to make them neat. Use a 3-inch biscuit cutter to cut out 4 rounds. Gather the dough scraps, roll them out just as you did before, and cut out 2 more rounds.

Set the dough rounds on the prepared cookie sheet, evenly spacing them apart. Bake until the shortcakes are golden brown on top, 18 to 20 minutes. Ask an adult to help you remove the cookie sheet from the oven and set it on a wire rack. Let the shortcakes cool while you prepare the strawberries.

To prepare the strawberries, put the berries on a cutting board. Ask an adult to help you cut out the stem and core from the center of each berry and cut the berries into wedges. Put the sliced berries in a medium bowl and sprinkle with the granulated sugar (the amount of sugar depends on how sweet the berries are—taste one!). Let the berries stand for 10 minutes.

To make the whipped cream, in a large bowl, using an electric mixer, beat the cream, granulated sugar, and vanilla on low speed until the cream begins to thicken and no longer splatters, about 2 minutes. Raise the mixer speed to medium-high and continue to beat until the cream forms peaks that droop slightly when the beaters are lifted (turn off the mixer first!), about 3 minutes.

Ask an adult to help you split each cooled shortcake in half horizontally. Place the shortcake bottoms, cut side up, on serving plates and spoon the strawberries on top, dividing them equally. Add a big spoonful of whipped cream and top with the shortcake tops. Put the powdered sugar in a fine-mesh sieve, hold it over each shortcake, and tap the side of the sieve to dust the shortcake with sugar. Serve right away.

Rocky Road Fudge

Just like the ice cream flavor, this rocky road fudge is chock-full of marshmallows and nuts. Choose your favorite type of nut or use colored marshmallows instead of white ones. Or, just leave out the nuts and marshmallows and make good ol' plain fudge.

½ teaspoon vegetable oil

3½ cups mini marshmallows

2 cups chopped toasted walnuts, almonds, or pecans

2 cups semisweet chocolate chips

1 (14-ounce) can sweetened condensed milk

1 teaspoon vanilla extract

Line an 8-inch square baking pan with aluminum foil, gently pressing the foil into the corners and letting the extra foil hang over the sides. Soak a paper towel with the vegetable oil and use it to rub over the foil. Set aside ½ cup of the mini marshmallows and ½ cup of the nuts.

Put the chocolate chips and condensed milk in a medium microwave-safe bowl. Ask an adult to help you microwave the mixture on high for 1 minute. Stir with a rubber spatula. If the chips aren't melted, return to the microwave 1 or 2 times for 30 seconds each, stirring after each time, just until the chocolate is melted. Don't let the chocolate get too hot!

Using a rubber spatula, gently stir the vanilla, the remaining 3 cups of mini marshmallows, and the remaining 1½ cups of the nuts into the chocolate mixture. Using the spatula, scrape the chocolate mixture into the prepared baking pan. Spread it evenly and smooth the top.

Sprinkle the fudge with the reserved marshmallows and nuts and gently press them into the surface. Cover the pan with plastic wrap and refrigerate until firm, at least 30 minutes.

Holding the ends of the foil, lift the fudge out of the pan and set it on a cutting board. Peel away the foil and ask an adult to help you cut the fudge into 16 squares.

Banana-Chocolate Chip Bread

This rich, moist bread is best when you use bananas that are overly ripe, because they are a lot softer and sweeter. Chocolate chips make this an extra-special version, but you can leave them out if you like or swap them out for chopped toasted pecans.

☆

2 cups all-purpose flour

2 teaspoons baking powder

½ teaspoon baking soda

¼ teaspoon salt

½ teaspoon ground cinnamon

⅛ teaspoon ground nutmeg

3 very ripe, large bananas, peeled and smashed

2 large eggs

1 cup firmly packed brown sugar

½ cup sour cream

1 teaspoon vanilla extract

4 tablespoons (½ stick) unsalted butter, melted

½ cup semisweet chocolate chips

Preheat the oven to 350°F. Generously butter a 9-by-5-inch loaf pan, then line it with a piece of parchment paper, extending it up and over the sides, and butter the parchment paper.

In a medium bowl, whisk together the flour, baking powder, baking soda, salt, cinnamon, and nutmeg. In a large bowl, whisk together the bananas, eggs, brown sugar, sour cream, vanilla, and butter. Add the flour mixture to the banana mixture and stir gently with a rubber spatula just until combined. Stir in the chocolate chips.

Scrape the batter into the prepared pan. Put the pan in the oven and bake until a toothpick inserted into the center of the loaf comes out clean (ask an adult for help!), about 1 hour.

Ask an adult to help you remove the pan from the oven and set it on a wire rack. Let cool in the pan for about 15 minutes, then, using the parchment, carefully lift the loaf out and place it onto the rack. Let cool completely.

Ask an adult to help you cut the bread into slices and serve.

Make muffins!
Just line a 12-cup muffin pan with liners, divide the banana bread batter between the cups, and bake for 18 minutes!

Blondie sundae

For a special treat, omit the glaze and top blondie squares with vanilla ice cream, hot fudge, and sliced almonds.

Caramel-Glazed Blondies

Blondies are like brownies, but they have a yummy brown-sugar flavor instead of chocolate and are lighter in color. These are covered in a sweet, creamy glaze to make them even more delicious! Bake them for your next sleepover.

BLONDIES

½ cup (1 stick) unsalted butter

1 cup firmly packed dark brown sugar

1½ cups all-purpose flour

1 teaspoon baking powder

¼ teaspoon salt

2 large eggs

1 teaspoon vanilla extract

CARAMEL GLAZE

¼ cup (½ stick) unsalted butter

¾ cup firmly packed dark brown sugar

½ cup heavy cream

1 teaspoon vanilla extract

½ cup powdered sugar, sifted

 Preheat the oven to 325°F. Line a 9-inch square baking pan with parchment paper, extending it up and over the sides on two sides.

To make the blondies, in a small saucepan, combine the butter and brown sugar. Ask an adult to help you set the pan over medium heat and warm the mixture, stirring often, until melted and smooth. Using a rubber spatula, scrape the mixture into a large bowl and let cool slightly.

In a small bowl, whisk together the flour, baking powder, and salt. Add the eggs and vanilla to the butter mixture and mix with a large spoon until smooth. Add the flour mixture and stir just until combined. Pour the batter into the prepared pan. Put the pan in the oven and bake until a toothpick inserted into the center comes out with moist crumbs attached (ask an adult for help!), 20 to 25 minutes. Ask an adult to help you remove the pan from the oven and set it on a wire rack. Let cool completely.

To make the glaze, in a saucepan, combine the butter, brown sugar, and cream. Ask an adult to help you set the pan over medium heat and warm the mixture, stirring, until melted. Raise the heat to medium-high and let the mixture boil for 2 minutes. Remove from the heat, stir in the vanilla, and let cool. Stir in the powdered sugar. Spread the glaze evenly over the blondies. Let stand until set.

Holding the ends of the parchment, lift the blondies onto a cutting board. Use a warm knife to cut into 16 squares and serve.

Blueberry Turnovers

You can fill these charming handheld pies with any kind of berry you like: sliced strawberries, raspberries, and blackberries all work well. They're perfect for taking on adventures because they're small and travel well.

TURNOVERS

1 sheet frozen puff pastry, thawed

2 cups blueberries

3 tablespoons granulated sugar

2 tablespoons all-purpose flour

½ teaspoon grated lemon zest

2 teaspoons lemon juice

1 large egg, lightly beaten

GLAZE

½ cup powdered sugar, sifted

1 tablespoon lemon juice

1 tablespoon orange juice

 Preheat the oven to 400°F. Line a cookie sheet with parchment paper.

To make the turnovers, unfold the puff pastry and place it on a clean work surface. Using a rolling pin, roll out the pastry to a square that's ⅛ inch thick. Cut the pastry into 3 equal strips, then cut the strips crosswise to make a total of 9 squares. Place the squares on the prepared baking sheet, spacing them apart evenly.

In a medium bowl, combine the berries, granulated sugar, flour, lemon zest, and lemon juice. Divide the berry mixture evenly among the pastry squares, placing it in the center of each square. Brush the edges of each square with the beaten egg. Fold each square on the diagonal to enclose the filling and form a triangle. Gently press along the edge with the back of the tines of a fork to seal in the filling. Put the cookie sheet in the oven and bake until the turnovers are golden brown, about 15 minutes. Ask an adult to help you remove the cookie sheet from the oven and set it on a wire rack. Let the turnovers cool completely.

To make the glaze, in a small bowl, whisk together the powdered sugar, lemon juice, and orange juice. Drizzle the glaze over the cooled turnovers. Let the glaze dry for about 15 minutes and serve.

Lemony Berry Bars

The easy press-in crust for these sweet-tart jam-filled bars is partly baked before you add the filling, to make sure that everything bakes up perfectly in the end.

CRUST

½ cup (1 stick) unsalted butter, at room temperature

1 cup all-purpose flour

¼ cup powdered sugar, sifted

1 tablespoon ice water

1 teaspoon vanilla extract

½ teaspoon salt

FILLING

¾ cup raspberry jam or other berry jam

6 large eggs

2 cups granulated sugar

¾ cup lemon juice

¼ cup all-purpose flour

¾ teaspoon baking powder

¼ teaspoon salt

½ cup powdered sugar, sifted

 Preheat the oven to 350°F. Grease a 9-inch square baking pan.

To make the crust, in a medium bowl, using an electric mixer, beat the butter on medium speed until creamy. Turn off the mixer. Add the flour, powdered sugar, ice water, vanilla, and salt and beat on low speed just until the mixture is well blended and forms small clumps that hold together when pressed between two fingers. Using clean hands, scoop the dough into the prepared pan and press to form an even layer in the bottom of the pan. Refrigerate for 10 minutes.

Put the pan in the oven and bake the crust until golden, about 15 minutes. Ask an adult to help you remove the pan from the oven and set it on a wire rack. Reduce the oven temperature to 325°F.

To make the filling, using a rubber spatula, ask an adult to help you carefully spread the jam evenly over the warm crust. In a medium bowl, whisk the eggs, granulated sugar, lemon juice, flour, baking powder, and salt until well combined. Pour the egg mixture over the jam-topped crust, carefully spreading it with the spatula to form an even layer.

Return the pan to the oven and bake until the filling doesn't jiggle when you gently shake the pan (ask an adult for help!), 40 to 45 minutes. Ask an adult to help you remove the pan from the oven and set it on a wire rack. Let cool, then transfer to the refrigerator to cool completely. Ask an adult to help you cut around the edges of the pan to loosen the sides; then cut the bars into small rectangles or squares. Just before serving, put the powdered sugar in a fine-mesh sieve and dust the bars with sugar.

Chocolate Truffles

If you love chocolate, these super choco-licious candies are for you! To give them as sweet little gifts to friends and family, put the truffles in colorful plastic bags and tie the bags with pretty ribbons or tuck them into candy cups and nestle them in a pretty box.

¼ cup heavy cream

4 tablespoons (½ stick) unsalted butter, cut into small pieces

8 ounces semisweet chocolate, chopped into small pieces

¼ teaspoon vanilla extract

¼ cup powdered sugar or unsweetened cocoa powder, sifted

In a saucepan over medium heat, warm the cream until tiny bubbles appear around the edges of the pan (ask an adult to help!). Turn off the heat. Add the butter and chocolate to the saucepan and stir with a rubber spatula until everything is melted and the mixture is smooth. If the chocolate doesn't seem to be melting, turn on the heat to medium and warm, stirring, just until the mixture is smooth. Don't let the mixture get too hot!

Let the mixture cool for about 15 minutes. Using the rubber spatula, stir in the vanilla and scrape the mixture into a shallow bowl. Cover the bowl with plastic wrap and refrigerate until the chocolate mixture is solid, at least 4 hours or overnight.

Using a melon baller, scoop the chocolate mixture to make rough balls the size of a gumball. (The mixture will be rather firm, so you may want to ask an adult to help with scooping.) Place each scoop of truffle mixture onto a large plate.

Put the powdered sugar or cocoa in a shallow bowl. (Powdered sugar will give the truffles an extra layer of sweetness. Cocoa will make the truffles intensely chocolaty.) Working with 1 truffle scoop at a time, use the palms of your hands to roll it into a smooth, round ball and return the ball to the plate. After rolling, put the balls in the bowl with the coating of your choice. Roll each truffle in the powdered sugar or cocoa until it is completely coated, then put in a serving dish. Cover and store the truffles in the refrigerator until you are ready to eat them or offer them.

Raspberry-Chocolate Tartlets

As cute as they are delicious, these dainty mini tarts are perfect for a tea party. The tartlet shells are baked in a muffin pan, then each one is layered with raspberry jam, melt-in-your-mouth chocolate, and fresh raspberries.

✩

TARTLET SHELLS

1 large egg yolk

3 tablespoons ice water

1 teaspoon vanilla extract

1¼ cups all-purpose flour

¼ cup granulated sugar

⅛ teaspoon salt

½ cup (1 stick) cold unsalted butter, cut into small pieces

FILLING

4 ounces semisweet chocolate, chopped

3 tablespoons unsalted butter

1 tablespoon light corn syrup

¼ cup raspberry jam

2 cups raspberries

Powdered sugar, for dusting (optional)

To make the tartlet shells, in a small bowl, whisk the egg yolk, ice water, and vanilla until combined. In a food processor, pulse together the flour, granulated sugar, and salt. Scatter the butter pieces over the dry ingredients and pulse until the mixture resembles coarse cornmeal. Add the egg yolk mixture and pulse just until the dough clumps together.

Transfer the dough to a clean work surface, pat it into a ball with your hands, and flatten into a disk. Wrap the disk tightly in plastic wrap and refrigerate until chilled and firm, at least 30 minutes or up to overnight.

Spray the cups of a standard 12-cup muffin pan with nonstick cooking spray.

Sprinkle a clean work surface with flour. Unwrap the dough disk and place it on the floured surface. Sprinkle the top of the dough with a little more flour. Flour a rolling pin and roll out the dough until it is about ⅛ inch thick. Sprinkle more flour under and over the dough as needed so it doesn't stick. Using a 4-inch round cookie cutter, cut out as many rounds as you can from the dough. Press the dough scraps together, re-roll, and cut out additional rounds. You should have a total of 12 rounds. Line each cup of the prepared muffin pan with a dough round, easing it in, then patting firmly into the bottom and up the sides of the cup. Once you've lined all the cups, freeze the tartlet shells in the pan until firm, about 30 minutes.

~ Continued on page 110 ~

Choco-cream pie

For sweet little cream tartlets, omit the jam and fresh fruit, fill the tartlets as directed, and top each with whipped cream.

~ Continued from page 109 ~

Place an oven rack in the lower third of the oven and preheat the oven to 375°F.

Place the pan in the oven and bake the tartlet shells until golden brown, about 15 minutes. Ask an adult to help you remove the pan from the oven and set it on a wire rack. Let cool completely, then carefully lift out the tartlet shells and set them on a large, flat serving plate to cool.

To make the filling, combine the chocolate, butter, and corn syrup in a medium microwave-safe bowl. Ask an adult to help you microwave the mixture on high heat, stirring every 20 seconds until it's melted and smooth. Don't let the chocolate mixture get too hot!

Spread ½ teaspoon of raspberry jam in the bottom of each cooled tartlet shell. Spoon in the chocolate mixture, dividing it evenly. Let the tartlets stand at room temperature to allow the chocolate to set, 1 to 2 hours.

Top each tartlet with raspberries. If you like, put some powdered sugar into a fine-mesh sieve, hold the sieve over the tartlets, and tap the side of the sieve to dust the tartlets with sugar. Serve right away.

Easy Cheesecake Pie

Who doesn't love smooth, creamy cheesecake in a crunchy graham cracker crust? Topped off with fresh, colorful berries (or other ripe summer fruit), this easy-to-make pie is perfect for a summertime party.

CRUST

15 graham crackers, broken into pieces

4 tablespoons (½ stick) unsalted butter, melted

3 tablespoons sugar

¼ teaspoon ground cinnamon

FILLING

2 (8-ounce) packages cream cheese, at room temperature

1 (14-ounce) can sweetened condensed milk

1 teaspoon finely grated lemon zest

3 tablespoons lemon juice

Mixed berries, for decorating (optional)

 Preheat the oven to 350°F. Put the graham crackers in a zippered plastic bag. Press out the air and seal the bag. Use a rolling pin to crush the crackers into fine crumbs, pounding them lightly or using a gentle back-and-forth rolling motion. Measure out 1¼ cups of crumbs.

To make the crust, in a bowl, combine the graham cracker crumbs, melted butter, sugar, and cinnamon. Stir with a wooden spoon until the crumbs are evenly moistened. Pour the crumb mixture into a 9-inch glass pie dish. Using your hands, press the crumbs into an even layer into the bottom and all the way up the sides of the dish. Put the pie dish in the oven and bake until the crust is firm, 6 to 7 minutes. Ask an adult to help you remove the pie dish from the oven and place it on a wire rack. Let cool completely, about 30 minutes.

To make the filling, in a large bowl, using an electric mixer, beat the cream cheese on medium speed until smooth, 2 to 3 minutes. Turn off the mixer. Add the condensed milk and beat until smooth, about 1 minute. Turn off the mixer and scrape down the bowl with a rubber spatula. Add the lemon zest and juice and beat until the mixture is smooth, about 30 seconds. Using the rubber spatula, scrape the filling into the cooled piecrust. Spread the filling out evenly and smooth the top. Refrigerate the pie until well chilled, about 3 hours.

If you like, top the pie with mixed berries. Ask an adult to help you cut the pie into wedges and serve.

Apple Oven Pancake

Unlike pancakes that you make on the stovetop, this is one big puffy pancake that bakes in the oven. Have an adult help you pour the batter over the apples in the hot pan, then watch through the oven door as the pancake puffs up like magic!

1 large baking apple, such as Gala or Granny Smith

4 tablespoons granulated sugar

½ teaspoon ground cinnamon

3 large eggs

1 cup whole milk

¾ cup all-purpose flour

¾ teaspoon vanilla extract

2 tablespoons powdered sugar

 Preheat the oven to 400°F. Butter a 9-inch glass pie dish.

Ask an adult to help you peel the apple, cut it into quarters, and remove the core from each quarter. Cut the apple quarters into small chunks.

In a medium bowl, using a fork, stir together 2 tablespoons of the granulated sugar and ¼ teaspoon of the cinnamon. Add the apple chunks and toss with the fork until the pieces are evenly coated with the cinnamon-sugar. Transfer the apple chunks to the prepared dish, spreading them out evenly with the fork.

In a blender, combine the remaining granulated sugar, the remaining cinnamon, the eggs, milk, flour, and vanilla. Put the lid on securely and blend on medium speed until the ingredients are well mixed and frothy, about 1 minute.

Put the pie dish in the oven and bake the apple chunks for 5 minutes. Ask an adult to help you pull out the oven rack just enough so that you can pour the batter evenly over the apples. Carefully slide the rack back into the oven and close the oven door. Bake the pancake until puffed and brown, about 25 minutes.

Ask an adult to help you remove the dish from the oven and set it on a wire rack. While the pancake is still warm, put the powdered sugar in a fine-mesh sieve. Hold the sieve over the pancake and dust the pancake with sugar. Ask an adult to help you cut the pancake into wedges and serve.

Cherry Crisp

A crisp is a baked fruit dessert with a sweet, crunchy topping of oats, flour, and sugar. This crisp is delicious on its own, but vanilla ice cream makes it totally irresistible!

TOPPING

4 tablespoons (½ stick) unsalted butter, at room temperature

¼ cup firmly packed light brown sugar

½ teaspoon ground cinnamon

Pinch of salt

½ cup old-fashioned oats

¼ cup all-purpose flour

FILLING

2 pounds frozen pitted cherries, thawed

1 teaspoon vanilla extract

½ cup granulated sugar

1 tablespoon cornstarch

Pinch of salt

Vanilla ice cream, for serving

To make the topping, in a medium bowl, using a wooden spoon, stir together the butter, brown sugar, cinnamon, and salt until combined. Stir in the oats and flour. Cover with plastic wrap and refrigerate while you make the filling.

Preheat the oven to 375°F. Butter a 2-quart glass baking dish.

To make the filling, set a colander over a bowl and put the cherries in the colander to drain off any liquid. Put the drained cherries in a large bowl, add the vanilla, and stir with a wooden spoon. Sprinkle in the granulated sugar, cornstarch, and salt and stir to combine.

Transfer the cherry mixture to the prepared baking dish and spread it out evenly. Remove the topping from the refrigerator and sprinkle it evenly over the fruit. Put the dish in the oven and bake, until the filling is bubbling and the topping is brown, 30 to 35 minutes.

Ask an adult to help you remove the dish from the oven and set it on a wire rack to cool for about 20 minutes.

To serve, scoop up portions of the warm crisp onto dessert plates. Top each serving with ice cream and serve right away.

Golden Layer Cake with Chocolate Frosting

This towering chocolate-frosted vanilla butter cake will make your friends and family say, "Wow!" Decorate it with your favorite colored sprinkles for a birthday, write a fun message on top with icing, or mound fresh raspberries onto the center.

CAKE

3 cups all-purpose flour

2 teaspoons baking powder

½ teaspoon salt

1 cup (2 sticks) unsalted butter, at room temperature

2 cups granulated sugar

4 large eggs

1 cup buttermilk

FROSTING

2 cups semisweet chocolate chips

½ cup (1 stick) unsalted butter, at room temperature

1 cup sour cream

2 teaspoons vanilla extract

5 cups powdered sugar, sifted

Sprinkles and/or candies, for decorating

Preheat the oven to 350°F. Trace the bottom of two 8-inch round cake pans onto sheets of parchment paper and cut out the circles with scissors. Rub the insides of the cake pans with a little butter. Put the paper circles in the bottom of the pans and butter the paper.

To make the cake, in a medium bowl, whisk together the flour, baking powder, and salt. In a large bowl, using an electric mixer, beat the butter and granulated sugar on medium-high speed until fluffy and pale, 3 to 4 minutes. Turn off the mixer and scrape down the bowl with a rubber spatula. Add 2 of the eggs to the butter mixture and beat on medium speed until well combined. Turn off the mixer. Add the remaining 2 eggs and beat on medium speed until well combined. Turn off the mixer and scrape down the bowl. Add half of the flour mixture and mix on low speed just until blended. Turn off the mixer. Pour in the buttermilk and mix on low speed just until blended. Turn off the mixer. Add the remaining flour mixture and mix just until blended. Turn off the mixer one last time and scrape down the bowl.

Divide the batter evenly between the cake pans and gently smooth the tops with the rubber spatula. Put the cake pans in the oven and bake until the cakes are golden brown and a wooden skewer inserted into the centers of the cakes comes out clean (ask an adult for help!), 45 to 50 minutes.

~ Continued on page 119 ~

~ *Continued from page 116* ~

Ask an adult to help you remove the cake pans from the oven and set them on wire racks. Let cool for 20 minutes, then run a table knife around the inside edge of each cake pan. Turn the pans over onto the racks. Lift away the pans and the parchment paper and let the cakes cool completely, upside down, about 2 hours.

To make the frosting, put the chocolate chips in a microwave-safe bowl. Ask an adult to help you microwave the chips on high heat, stirring every 20 seconds until they are melted and smooth. Don't let the chocolate get too hot!

In a large bowl, using the electric mixer, beat the butter, sour cream, and vanilla until smooth. Add the melted chocolate and beat until smooth. With the electric mixer on low speed, beat in the powdered sugar ½ cup at a time. When all of the sugar has been added, raise the speed to high and beat until the frosting is nice and smooth. Scrape down the bowl with the spatula and beat for 1 minute more.

When the cakes have cooled, place one layer on a cake stand or plate. Using an offset spatula, spread some of the frosting over the top, nearly to the edge, making a thick layer as even as possible. Place the second cake layer on top of the frosting, trying to line up the sides of the cakes. Spread more frosting over the top of the cake and down the sides, creating a thick layer. Decorate the cake with sprinkles and/or candies.

Serve the cake right away or cover it loosely with plastic wrap and refrigerate for up to 3 days. Ask an adult to help you cut the cake into wedges for serving.

Cake 'n' ice cream

Serve slices of the cake with big scoops of your favorite ice cream for an extra-special treat!

Index

weldonowen

1045 Sansome Street, Suite 100
San Francisco, CA 94111
www.weldonowen.com

Weldon Owen is a division of Bonnier Publishing USA

WELDON OWEN, INC.
President & Publisher Roger Shaw
VP, Sales & Marketing Amy Kaneko
Finance & Operations Director Philip Paulick

Associate Publisher Amy Marr
Project Editor Kim Laidlaw
Associate Editor Emma Rudolph

Creative Director Kelly Booth
Designer Alexandra Zeigler
Production Designer Monica S. Lee

Production Director Chris Hemesath
Associate Production Director Michelle Duggan

Photographer Nicole Hill Gerulat
Food Stylists Tara Bench, Robyn Valarik
Prop Stylists Veronica Olson, Leigh Noe
Hair & Makeup Kathy Hill

AMERICAN GIRL *BAKING*
Conceived and produced by Weldon Owen, Inc.
In collaboration with Williams Sonoma, Inc.
3250 Van Ness Avenue, San Francisco, CA 94109

A WELDON OWEN PRODUCTION

Printed and bound by RR Donnelley in China

First printed in 2015
20 19 18 17 16 15 14 13 12 11 10

Library of Congress Cataloging in Publication
data is available

ISBN 13: 978-1-68188-022-8
ISBN 10: 1-68188-022-9

ACKNOWLEDGMENTS
Weldon Owen wishes to thank the following people for their generous support
to help produce this book: Laura Bee, Marie Bench, Mary Bench, David Bornfriend,
Peggy Fallon, Amy Machnak Hash, Taylor Olson, A'Lissa Olson, Abby Stolfo, and Cassidy Tuttle

A VERY SPECIAL THANK YOU TO:
Our models: Avenlie Fullmer, Abigail Holtby, Sophia Jarque,
Swayzie King, Jane Robinson, Eden Rosenthal, and Kaia Sperry

Our locations: The Copes, The Williamsons, and The Wilsons

Our party resources: Oh Happy Day Shop, Shop Sweet Lulu, and Sweetapolita

Our clothing resources: Rachel Riley (rachelriley.com) and Tea Collection (teacollection.com)